PENGUINS!
STRANGE AND WONDERFUL

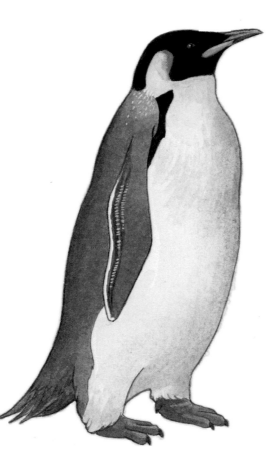

Laurence Pringle   Illustrated by **Meryl Henderson**

BOYDS MILLS PRESS
AN IMPRINT OF HIGHLIGHTS
Honesdale, Pennsylvania

In memory of Randall James Falk, who believed that life is all about showing up, laughing, and looking good in a tux—and who always said that only penguins truly know how to dress for success!

—LP

To Sue and Andy Cowan: Sue's parakeet Indigo was the first of several delightful birds in my life.

—MH

Thanks to Wayne Trivelpiece, PhD, director of research for the United States Antarctic Marine Living Resources Program, and Doug Wechsler, director of VIREO (Visual Resource for Ornithology, part of The Academy of Natural Sciences), for their assistance in the development of this book.

Text copyright © 2007 by Laurence Pringle
Illustrations copyright © 2007 by Meryl Henderson

For information about permission to reproduce selections from this book, please contact permissions@highlights.com.

Boyds Mills Press, Inc.
An Imprint of Highlights
815 Church Street
Honesdale, Pennsylvania 18431
Printed in China

Library of Congress Cataloging-in-Publication Data

Pringle, Laurence P.
  Penguins! strange and wonderful / by Laurence Pringle ; illustrated by Meryl Henderson.— 1st ed.
      p. cm.
  Includes bibliographical references.
  ISBN-13: 978-1-59078-090-9 (hc) · ISBN: 978-1-62091-591-2 (pb)
  1. Penguins—Juvenile literature. I. Henderson, Meryl, ill. II. Title.

  QL696.S473P75 2007
  598.47—dc22

2006000521

First paperback edition, 2013
The text of this book is set in Clearface Regular.
The illustrations are done in watercolor.

10 9 8 7 6 5 4 3 2 1

In the year 1520, explorers from Portugal sailed near the coast of South America. They saw strange black-and-white birds that could dive, swim, and leap out of the water but could not fly.

The explorers called these birds "strange geese." Today we call them penguins.

Magellanic penguins

People love penguins! They love the funny way penguins waddle along on land. They love the way penguins look: standing very straight in black and white, like little people dressed up for a formal wedding or a fancy party.

There are seventeen kinds, or species, of penguins on Earth. They are all alike in some ways. All penguins live in the southern half of the world, the Southern Hemisphere. All penguins are flightless birds that spend most of their lives at sea. All penguins have dark backs and white fronts.

Chinstrap penguins

Little blue penguins

Nevertheless, penguins differ a lot in size, in looks, and in the places they live. If you imagine a penguin, you probably picture it surrounded by snow and ice. You might imagine the biggest penguin of all, the emperor penguin of Antarctica. It stands almost four feet tall.

You probably did not think of the little blue penguin, which stands just sixteen inches tall. This smallest of all penguins lives along the coasts of southern Australia and southern New Zealand. It hops ashore into green forests, not snow and ice.

Emperor penguins with chicks

Scientists who study birds have arranged all of the penguins on Earth into six groups, shown here. They differ in size, but the most noticeable differences are markings and feathers on their heads and upper chests. For example, six species all have long yellow or orange feathers on their heads that look like crests or bushy eyebrows. They form a group called the crested penguins.

Crested Penguins

erect-crested   *fiordland*   *macaroni*   *rockhopper*   *royal*   *Snares Island*

There are four species of penguins that have a single or double black band across their upper chests.

Banded Penguins

black-footed   *Galapagos*   *Humboldt*   *Magellanic*

Three kinds of penguins have tails that are longer than the tails of other species. They are called the brush-tailed or stiff-tailed penguins.

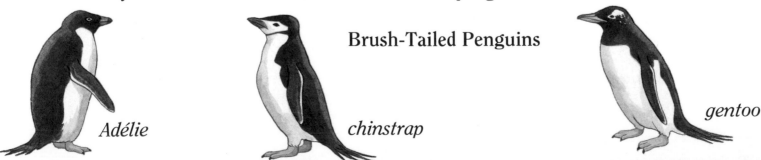

Brush-Tailed Penguins

Adélie   *chinstrap*   *gentoo*

The two biggest penguins are alike in many ways and so are classified in a separate group.

Giant Penguins

emperor

king

Two other species of penguins are not closely related to any of the others or to each other.

little blue

yellow-eyed

As you can see by looking at all of the penguin species on these pages, some are named for the way they look. Others, like the Snares Island penguin and the Galapagos penguin, are named for the places in which they live. The Adélie penguin is named after a place in Antarctica—Terre Adélie (Adélie Land)—that French explorer Jules Dumont d'Urville had named after his wife.

Penguins are scattered far and wide in the Southern Hemisphere. Adélie and emperor penguins live the farthest south of all, in Antarctica. Galapagos penguins live more than three thousand miles away, in a tropical climate at the equator.

This map is like a view from space, with Antarctica directly below, and parts of Africa, South America, and Australia in the distance. A small penguin symbol marks the islands and coasts of continents where all sorts of penguins live. As the list below shows, as many as four species can be found in some places, and some penguins have more than one common name.

Where Penguins Live

Adélie Penguin: Antarctica and Bouvet, South Orkney, South Sandwich, and South Shetland islands

Black-footed (Jackass) Penguin: southern Africa

Chinstrap Penguin: Antarctic Peninsula and Bouvet, Heard, South Georgia, South Orkney, South Sandwich, and South Shetland islands

Emperor Penguin: Antarctica

Erect-crested Penguin: Antipodes, Auckland, Bounty, and Campbell islands

Fiordland Penguin: South Island of New Zealand

Galapagos Penguin: Galápagos Islands

Gentoo Penguin: Antarctic Peninsula and Bouvet, Crozet, Falkland, Heard, Kerguelen, Macquarie, Marion, South Georgia, South Orkney, South Shetland, and Staten islands

Humboldt (Peruvian) Penguin: southwestern coast of South America and small islands off Peru

King Penguin: Crozet, Heard, Falkland, Kerguelen, Macquarie, Marion, South Georgia, South Sandwich, and Staten islands

Little Blue (Fairy) Penguin: Tasmania, southern Australia, and South Island of New Zealand

Macaroni Penguin: Antarctic Peninsula and Bouvet, Falkland, Heard, Kerguelen, Prince Edward, South Georgia, South Orkney, South Sandwich, and South Shetland islands

Magellanic Penguin: Falkland and Staten islands and southern South America, especially Punta Tombo in southern Argentina

Rockhopper Penguin: southern South America and Amsterdam, Antipodes, Auckland, Bounty, Campbell, Crozet, Falkland, Gough, Kerguelen, Macquarie, Prince Edward, St. Paul, Snares, and Tristan da Cunha islands

Royal Penguin: Macquarie Island

Snares Island Penguin: Snares Islands (south of New Zealand)

Yellow-eyed Penguin: South Island of New Zealand and Auckland, Campbell, and Stewart islands

Punta
Tomb

*SOUTH
AMERICA*

← Galápagos

AFRICA

Tristan da Cunha
Gough I.

ATLANTIC OCEAN

Bouvet I.

Greenwich Meridian

Prince Edward Is.

Marion I.

South Sandwich Is.

Crozet Is.

South Georgia Is.

Falkland Is.

South
Orkney Is.

Staten Is.

Weddell
Sea

Kerguelen Is.

South
Shetland Is.

Heard I.

ANTARCTICA

Amsterdam I.
St. Paul I.

90° W

Peter I.

90° E

INDIAN OCEAN

Antarctic Circle

PACIFIC OCEAN

Ross Sea

Balleny Is.

Macquarie I.

Campbell I.

Auckland Is.

Antipodes Is.
Bounty Is.

Snares Is.

Stewart I.

TASMANIA

Chatham Is.

South I.

NEW
ZEALAND

AUSTRALIA

North I.

Galapagos penguins

Wherever they live, penguins are awkward on land but graceful and swift in the water. Their bodies are streamlined, like torpedoes, and water flows easily over their densely packed scale-like feathers. Their short wings, or flippers, flap up and down with great power. Penguins steer with their short tails and their feet. They are agile in the water, able to change direction in an instant.

Birds that fly have lightweight, hollow bones. Penguin bones are solid and heavy. This helps them swim and dive. Penguins come close to flight only when they leap out of the water—as high as six feet—onto land or ice, or when they travel by "porpoising." Fast-moving penguins leap completely out of the water, as porpoises do, every few seconds. They take a quick breath and dive back in. Porpoising penguins can zoom along at twenty-five miles an hour for short distances. They usually travel at a slower pace but still cover vast distances. Some species live in different ocean waters in summer and winter and swim several thousand miles each year.

Macaroni penguins porpoising

The biggest penguins are the fastest swimmers and the deepest divers. Emperor penguins can swim up to nine miles an hour—twice the speed of the fastest human swimmers. Emperors can dive more than seventeen hundred feet below the surface and stay underwater for eighteen minutes. Most of the time, though, penguins stay submerged for a minute or two, and they don't need to dive far in order to catch some food.

Penguins are predators. Underwater they hunt for fish, squid, and crustaceans, including shrimplike krill. Penguins have no teeth, but their tongues and roofs of their mouths are covered with stiff spines that help grip slippery prey. Sometimes a penguin finds a school of hundreds of fish or a swarm of millions of krill. It may circle its prey, causing the animals to bunch together. Then the penguin strikes from below. In a few minutes it can catch and swallow a hundred krill or many small fish.

Rockhopper penguin

Emperor penguins hunting squid

Penguins spend month after month at sea. In the waters off New Zealand, barnacles begin to grow on the tail feathers of fiordland penguins (as they do on whales) that never leave the water. Penguins rest while floating on the surface. Wherever they swim, the water is cold. Even Galapagos penguins, which live close to the equator, swim in the cold Humboldt Current that flows northward from the Antarctic.

A coat of small, scale-like feathers helps protect penguins from the cold. The feathers overlap to form a watertight surface. Whether at sea or on land, penguins spend some time each day taking care of their feathers. They reach back to an oil gland at the base of their tails, rub some oil onto their beaks, then spread the oil over their feathers. This helps keep the feathers waterproof.

When penguins are well fed, a layer of fat grows beneath their skin. The stored fat is an energy reserve, and it also helps protect the birds from the cold. Adélie and emperor penguins of Antarctica face the greatest challenge of cold temperatures. The Adélie has feathers covering half of its beak. The emperor has feathers covering its legs. In contrast, penguins that live in warmer places sometimes need to lose heat to avoid overheating. They have bare beaks and legs. Some species even have bare skin on their faces.

King penguins
swimming

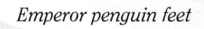

Emperor penguin feet

Adélie
penguin

Chinstrap penguin preening

Magellanic
penguin

Penguins are such super swimmers they could live year-round in the sea. However, they must come ashore to raise their young and to grow a new coat of feathers. They stay close to the sea because they need to be near a supply of food and because they cannot walk fast on their short legs. Rockhopper penguins are named for their ability to jump up or down rocky hillsides. Penguins that live in snowy places sometimes flop on their bellies and push themselves with their wings. They slide along faster than they can walk. This is called tobogganing.

In mating season, most penguin species gather in large groups and nest close together. However, the nests of little blue penguins are spaced far apart, hidden under bushes, in rocky crevices, or in short burrows that the penguins dig.

Yellow-eyed penguins are even less sociable. If a pair of these penguins can see the nest of a neighboring pair, they usually try to find a more private place in the New Zealand forest.

Rockhopper penguins

Gentoo penguins
tobogganing

Yellow-eyed penguins

In September and October—spring in the Southern Hemisphere—many penguin species gather in colonies, or rookeries, made up of hundreds or thousands or sometimes millions of birds! A penguin colony is a lively, noisy, smelly place. Male penguins usually come ashore first. Each one tries to claim a good nesting place. Sometimes fights break out. Two males bash with their tough flippers and peck with their sharp beaks until one gives up and retreats. Then the winner makes loud calls. Other males join in. The air fills with loud penguin calls.

Each species of penguin has a distinctive voice. The black-footed penguin is often called the jackass penguin because its hee-haw voice sounds like a jackass or donkey. Its closest relatives, the Galapagos, Humboldt, and Magellanic penguins, make similar noises. Other kinds of penguins croak, squawk, bleat, bark, or trumpet.

The loud noises of a penguin colony are matched only by its powerful smells. Penguin poop, called guano, is sprayed wherever the birds walk and especially around every nest where they spend much of their time on land. The color of a penguin's guano often reveals what it ate. If the guano is white or gray, the food was fish; yellow, it was squid; pink, it was krill.

Male black-footed (jackass) penguins fighting

Gentoo penguin rookery

*Magellanic penguins
in front of their burrow*

Royal penguins courting

When penguins court, a male and a female often stand close together, point their beaks toward the sky, and call loudly. Pairs of some species click their beaks together and bow. Once they have mated, both birds help raise their young.

Most nest building is done by the males. All penguins except kings and emperors make some sort of nest—in a burrow, another sheltered place, or out in the open. Penguins that live in hot climates must protect their eggs and young from the heat. Galapagos and Humboldt penguins often nest in caves and crevices near the shore. Little blue penguins line their burrow nests with grass and seaweed. Magellanic penguins also nest in burrows and may add bones and even the skin and feathers of dead penguins to their nests.

The penguins of colder climates build their nests on top of soil or rocks. On the coldest lands of all, chinstrap, gentoo, and Adélie penguins build nests of pebbles. The piles of little stones keep the eggs a few inches above the ground and protect them from being flooded by water from melted snow. A male penguin is always on the lookout for more pebbles to add to its nest. He may snatch one from an unguarded nest and then quickly carry it home.

Adélie nests are built close to one another, and a penguin defends its nest territory against any intruder. It may give a passing penguin a sharp peck. When a penguin needs to walk near other nests, it moves quickly with its beak held high and its wings tight against its sides, trying to make itself as skinny as possible. This is called the "slender walk."

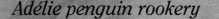

Adélie penguin rookery

A female Adélie penguin lays two eggs about three days apart. Then she leaves for about two weeks to hunt for food in the sea. Her mate keeps the eggs warm with his body, turning them so they are heated evenly. He eats nothing. When she returns, he goes for food while she warms the eggs. They continue to take turns for about thirty-five days, when chicks hatch from the eggs. Then the parents take turns getting food for their young. When a parent returns to the nest with a full stomach, it opens its beak. A chick reaches in. The parent coughs up, or regurgitates, some food that is partially digested. The chick gobbles it down.

Adélie penguins

Skua

Baby penguins are covered with downy feathers. For a while they still need to be kept warm by a parent. They also must be guarded. Predatory birds called skuas visit rookeries of Adélie, gentoo, and several other kinds of penguins. The skuas are hunting for food for themselves and their own young. They try to grab eggs or chicks. Penguin parents try to drive skuas away, striking them with their flippers and pecking with their beaks.

Wherever penguins live, they must defend their eggs or chicks from predators. Giant petrels, sheathbills, and several kinds of gulls prey on penguin colonies. In warmer climates, such animals as foxes, mongooses, snakes, and pigs raid penguin colonies. And in the Galápagos, Sally Lightfoot crabs sometimes carry off newly hatched chicks.

King penguins about to transfer an egg

In the spring, more than a million king penguins raise their young on South Georgia Island. They build no nests. Instead, the male and female take turns holding a single egg on top of their feet. It is kept warm with a special warm area of their belly skin called the brood patch. Emperors are the most unusual of all penguins in raising their young. They never set foot on land. And a bitterly cold winter lies ahead when they come onto thick Antarctic ice to mate. The mother lays a single large egg. She passes it to the father, who holds it on top of his feet and warms it with his brood patch. Then the mother leaves. She may walk or toboggan more than a hundred miles to find unfrozen water where she can dive in and hunt for food. The father waits, and waits, and waits—in the coldest, windiest place on Earth.

Living in a colony helps the male emperors survive. They huddle together and share the heat from their bodies. They move a bit, taking turns in the center of the group, where it is warmer. They turn their eggs, keeping them evenly heated. And they get thinner and thinner, sometimes losing half of their weight before the mothers return.

Usually the chicks hatch before the mothers get back. The chicks cuddle for warmth on top of their fathers' feet and get their food—special "crop milk"—from their fathers' mouths. The mothers soon arrive with full stomachs. They are ready to take the chicks from the fathers, keep them warm, and feed them. The fathers set out to catch some much-needed food. Both parents take turns bringing food to their young. The chicks begin to grow into penguins that will be able to take care of themselves in the Antarctic spring.

Huddle of male emperors

Emperor with chick

As chicks grow, a penguin colony is a lively place. After a month or so, most chicks are big enough to defend themselves. Both parents may leave to get more food for their hungry chicks. Parents hurry back and forth. When a returning parent calls out, its young recognize the voice and call back. They are fed only by their own parents.

In some penguin species, the young leave their nests and gather in a large group, called a creche. Chicks of Adélie, chinstrap, emperor, king, and rockhopper penguins do this. The chicks of king penguins form the largest creches of all—clusters of as many as a thousand birds in their scruffy coats of brown feathers.

Eventually all penguin chicks lose their coat of downy feathers. Under it lies their first sleek adult coat. This change is called molting. Adult penguins also molt, after their young are on their own, and must stay out of the water for several weeks while their new feathers grow in.

Chick molting

Creche of rockhopper chicks

Once young penguins have finished molting, they are ready to dive, swim, and hunt for their own food. They also swim into danger. Lurking in the sea are several kinds of animals that eat penguins, young and old.

Sharks, killer whales, sea lions, fur seals, and leopard seals often swim offshore of a penguin colony. They sometimes catch adult penguins that are returning with food. Young penguins on their first swim are easy prey. Leopard seals are especially dangerous. Sometimes they swim below a penguin that is walking on thin ice, then smash through the ice to grab it. In one day, a leopard seal can eat a dozen Adélie penguins.

Most penguins escape. They dart, leap, or dive out of danger. As they streak along at the surface, porpoising, penguins can change direction in the air. This may cause a seal or other predator to lose sight of them.

Leopard seal hunting Adélie penguins

Killer whale hunting yellow-eyed penguins

For millions of years, penguin populations have survived attacks by skuas, leopard seals, and other predators. They aren't doing nearly as well against Earth's most dangerous animals: humans. Early explorers killed penguins for food. Eventually, selling penguin eggs and meat became a big business in Africa and South America. People also learned that the stored fat of penguins could be "cooked" to yield oil. Countless penguins were used for this purpose. In 1867, for example, a company produced fifty thousand gallons of oil from the bodies of four hundred thousand king penguins.

Penguin numbers dropped very low in some areas. Scientists and ordinary people who cared about penguins fought to save them. They are now protected by laws, and the numbers of some species have grown. Nevertheless, ten of the seventeen species are listed as threatened, or in real danger of extinction.

Water pollution and especially oil spills harm penguins. Drift nets set in the ocean for fish catch penguins and cause them to drown. Overfishing of anchovies off the coasts of Africa and South America has robbed penguins of vital food.

This has caused the numbers of black-footed and Humboldt penguins to fall. Cutting down forests has destroyed nesting places of yellow-eyed and little blue penguins. Even well-meaning tourists harm penguins by disturbing their nesting colonies.